KITTI NEUMANN

I0492846

Online Business from Scratch

The 9 Step Guide to Building a Profitable and Sustainable Online Business

KITTI NEUMANN

KITTI NEUMANN

CONTENTS

KITTI NEUMANN

Introduction

First and foremost, I want to thank you for buying this book. You have really taken the first step to becoming a successful online entrepreneur.

Why should you read this book until the end of it?

I have done my best to finally make a book that summarizes all the information that every online entrepreneur needs to know when they start an online business. I personally studied all these things for years. So I made the decision that I would write a book with all the information in one place.

This book has lots of actionable information that you can use to build your own online business from scratch or make your existing business more profitable. However, this is not "DFY" (done for you). It is a guide with all the most important strategies to create an online business that makes you passive income. You need to take action after you read this book.

Today the internet provides us with a lot of opportunities. Maybe you saw more people who can afford to work from home or even travel the world without having a 9-5 job. How can they do this? The answer is: with the internet. This is an opportunity, and I believe you should live with it.

Do you want a life where you're free to do whatever you want? Do you want a life without a 9-5 job with no boss? Well, the best way to live the life you want is to start a business that earns you a passive income. All you need is a laptop and internet access.

Okay, so how can this book help you with getting started?

First of all, I'll help you to evolve the right mindset and philosophy because there are so many cases where people fail to build a successful online business. Why? The first chapter will be about this.

Then you need to find your customers because you can't sell to everybody. Who are they? This is your niche.

If you'd like to make tons of money, not just some sales here and there, you need a brand. I will explain this in the third chapter.

That's great. However, you can have the most perfect product/service, the most perfect website, but if you don't have traffic, it's all useless. So then I'll give you some tips to get traffic. If you have traffic, you need to turn your visitors into customers and then repeat buyers. This requires the right strategy. You can find this strategy in the fifth chapter, How To Create An Online Business.

Every successful long-term business is about adding value and being helpful to their customers. Without that, your business will die. I believe this is the most important part of this book. This is a must in every business.

These are the core strategies, but I'll give you some practical tips too. In the seventh chapter, we'll discuss the marketing tips to get more customers and earn a lot more money. If you use these tips, you'll get a big traffic tsunami. The more traffic, the more customers, the more money you make.

In the eighth chapter, I'll write some examples of online money making opportunities. This will give you a big picture of online business models.

The ninth chapter is a more advanced lesson. This will be useful once you have gone through all the previous lessons and applied them to your online business. The same for the last chapter, which is a bonus section for people who want to learn more and committed enough to work hard for their dreams.

Step 1: Why Do You Want To Build An Online Business And Why Do People Fail To Build One Successfully?

First, let me ask you a question. What does your dream life look like? Imagine that you're totally free. You don't have a 9-5 job, you don't have a boss. You can live wherever you want. You can do whatever you want. Imagine that. What would you do? You're able to travel the world, or you can spend all your time with your family. What is the most important thing to you? Please don't just read these questions, answer them too. Why do I ask these silly questions? Because building an online business requires hard work. So you need a 'why'. You need something that can motivate you when you have failures or just simply have a hard time. So first you need to know why you want to build an online business, what is your goal with it? It can be anything that can motivate you.

But why an online business? Today's world is all about technology and the internet. In fact, building an online business is easier, cheaper, and more profitable than building an offline business. You don't have to rent an office and pay a lot of money for offline advertising. You can start your own business with very little cost. However, you'll be able to make much more money than in an offline business in a much shorter period of time.

Last but not least, an online business can create a passive income so that you can live free. An online business can be automated. I think this is the most attractive reason. You might have to do some work with it, but you can work from wherever you want.

That's enough. I'm sure you already know what the advantages of building an online business are if you bought this book. So let's go over the next question, why do people fail to build a successful online business?

Well, there are several reasons for this. These include:

Being impatient

First, I want to clarify that failure isn't a bad thing. Failure is a natural thing and an opportunity to learn from your mistakes. Every successful person has failed and struggled at some point. Being successful is not easy. If it were easy, everybody would be successful.

I know you have seen many ads about making millions without any work or any time. But that's not the reality. If you want to build something successful, you have to be patient. It isn't a fast process. Just think about a few successful people. They failed sometimes but they never gave up, that's why they achieved their goals. While some people give up when they encounter obstacles, the successful people stand up and learn from their mistakes.

Lack of commitment

Secondly, you need to do a lot of work to be successful. You have to put in the work. I don't care if you have a full-time job, I don't care if you have no time. Find a way to work as much on your online business as possible. If your goal is strong enough, I'm sure you can put in the work. You cannot afford to be lazy.

An online business is more than just getting your goods onto a platform. It would be wise to remember that technology is a tool. It is not the endgame. It does not just allow you to showcase your business but it must be controlled by a human being. This means that you have to commit your time and energy. Make no mistake. Starting a business has physical, mental, emotional and financial implications. If you're not committed, you'll lose sight of your goal and before you know it, you'll be doing something else. That will not help your cause.

Having no marketing plan

This goes hand in hand with lack of commitment. Many online businesses fail because they underestimate the work they need to do to establish themselves. As we've said, technology gives your business a platform. It does not make business decisions for you. If you want to sell your stuff, you must create a marketing plan that will allow you to reach your customers.

You have to ask yourself the tough questions. What are you selling? Who are you selling it too? Where can you find your target customers? How can you convince them to buy your product? You also have to ask yourself how much time and cash you're willing to spend on marketing your product.

Comparison

Comparison is a trap many online business owners fall into. They look into what others are doing and start feeling discouraged because they have not achieved the same level of success. Here is the thing. When it comes to creating your online business, you have to start from scratch and grow at your own pace. If you concentrate on what others are doing, you will spend more time breeding self-doubt and worry instead of growing your brand. You need to focus on your business.

My advice is to have faith. You have to believe that you can do it. Read success stories. Find people who have already achieved what you want. If they can make it, you can make it too. Your goal should be to learn what you could from them ad not setting impossible standards for yourself. As most successful people will tell you, you need to have faith in the process. It's not a scam, it works. If you have faith, you will take action and taking action is the key to building a successful online business.

Okay, so commit yourself and think long-term. You won't be successful and rich by tomorrow. However, if you start working on your business today, you will be thankful for it even a year later. I will show you the map, the strategies, but you must work hard and take action.

Step 2: What Is Your Passion? Finding Your Niche

A niche is a segment, a market that you need to focus on. A niche has people with the same needs and wants. Your task as an internet marketer is to satisfy their needs. If you want to fulfill them successfully, you need to inquire about this topic. That's why you need to answer the following questions. What is your passion? What is your hobby? What do you do in your free time? It must be something that you love to learn, that you're passionate about.

The three biggest niches are health, money, and relationships. These are the three biggest areas that people have problems with. However, it doesn't mean that you have to choose from them. You really need something that you're passionate about. Remember, you need to focus on the long-term, not the short-term. If you choose a topic what you don't care, that's not long-term thinking. Try to find something that you enjoy studying. The best thing would be to teach while you learn.

Every business has a niche. Offline businesses are based around a niche too. You can't sell to everybody, because every person is different and they have different difficulties and pains. You can find subniches too, which are more narrow. This allows you to help people and focus on a more concrete topic.

Okay, so if you're interested in a topic and you choose that as a niche, you'll have an advantage. Find something that you would learn anyway. You can improve yourself and your niche too this way. However, do research before you commit yourself to a niche. Do a search on Google, YouTube or Amazon. Try to find forums and blogs, Facebook groups related to this niche. If you can find a few, it means that the niche has a market.

If you've found your niche, create your avatar. Your avatar is an imagined person in that certain niche. Write down everything about this person. What does the average day look like? What is their pain, their attitude? How old are they? What is the gender? Do they have a family? Are they married? Do they have children? If yes, how many? So write down everything. Having your avatar is very important to know because you'll have to find the right people, and your avatar will help you with that.

Some examples for niches include arts & entertainment, business/investing, computers/internet, sports, travel, cooking, education, self-help, health & fitness, parenting & families, politics, spirituality, languages, home & garden, employment & jobs, and so on.

Some examples for subniches in health & fitness include beauty, sleep& dreams, meditation, spiritual health, diets & weight loss, nutrition, remedies, exercise & fitness, and yoga. You can narrow your niche for men or just for women so that your niche can be men's health or women's health. Some examples for subniches in self-help include dating, eating disorder, marriage & relationship, time management, success, self-esteem, stress management, motivation, and public speaking.

The exercise for this chapter is to answer the questions at the beginning of this chapter and write down some of your ideas. Choose the niche that you are most interested about. After that, create your avatar, your ideal customer. Write down everything about him/her. You can even give him/her a name. You will use this avatar later when you plan your marketing.

Step 3: Build Your Brand

If you want to be successful and want to think long-term, you need a brand. A brand is a name. This name is related to your niche. You can have a website/blog or social media platforms, a podcast for your branding. Your logo is also related to your brand.

Why do you need a brand? A brand can create trust, credibility, likeability, and awareness. If you'd have a chance to choose, which product would you buy? A simple cola drink with no name behind it or Coca-Cola? You can more likely trust a product/or service with a brand behind it and you are more likely to buy that product. Or think about Apple. Apple is a brand. Moreover, Apple is all about the brand. Apple fans are loyal to the brand. Many people say "without the brand, Apple would be dead". Apple is not about computers or mobile devices, it's a passion. A brand has a value, it's very important.

The goal is to keep in touch with your customer. Don't let them forget you. You need to build trust and likeability. Create a website or blog, or you can use some of the social media platforms to keep in touch with your visitors. Creating content is not just for selling. By creating content, you can attract people to you. We live in a world where you can find content everywhere. Content is king. If you provide value, people are going to buy from you, because they know that you can help them. They know you, they trust you. Content can help you create a brand.

Your goal is not to build a business, your goal is to build a brand. Your goal is not to sell as many products as you can, your goal is to build a brand. You need to help to your customers. By building a brand, you can sell anything. Customers have feelings and emotion for brands. The most successful businesses have a brand. That's the key. That's the long-term. If you want your business to grow and become sustainable, you need a brand. The other advantage of building a brand is to other people can't complete with you.

Okay, so how can you build a brand? Well, you need to do a number of things to build a brand such as:

Choose a name

First, you need to choose a name. Don't try to be a perfectionist with that, but choose something that explains your vision. However, you need to be careful. Many times businesses don't stay the same. They tend to grow and go in other directions. You may start by offering one type of product and end up offering other types of products.

Thus, you have to be careful not to select a name that will prove limiting even as your business grows. Back to the example of Amazon, the name would have been very limiting indeed if it had been something like 'online books'. This is because the business expanded to include other products.

Next, you need to make sure that your chosen name is available. Remember, you're conducting an online business. This means you will need a website as well as social media channels. It would look very unprofessional if your various networks have different urls. This is why you need to conduct an online search to see if the name is available. You can check to see if you can get the domain name and platforms such YouTube, twitter, Facebook and instagram and whatever other platform you think you will need.

Another thing you can do is conduct a trademark search. You never know how big your business will become. You may need to protect yourself from competitors. A trademark offers you legal protection from those who would want to imitate your products or business. Further, don't forget to get some feedback from friends and family before deciding on a name.

Create a website

You can easily create a website. First, you need a hosting account like Bluehost and a domain name. Bluehost is really an inexpensive option. Your domain's name is your site's URL. Bluehost can give you a free domain name. However, you can buy your own domain name for example on GoDaddy too. Then you can set up a WordPress account, which is very easy to use. WordPress is a free blogging platform, and you can use it to create your website. Most websites run on WordPress. Anyone can set this up. It's really fast and inexpensive.

But before your website goes live, ensure that it meets your standards. Let's put it this way. Your website is often the first thing potential customers see when they stumble on your online business. It can put them off or make them want to learn more. It has to create a good impression. You'll want to introduce yourself to your visitors, let them know who you are and what you have to offer and how they can contact you. You can create static pages showcasing your business or you can have a blog to connect with your customers or, you can have both static pages and a blog.

Whatever you decide, be professional about it.

Create your identity

Your online business identity can make or break you. It determines how others perceive your business. Your identity starts with your name and your logo. It also includes your slogan and how you interact with visitors. Yes, your tone matters. Will you be friendly or professional? Will you strive for a picture perfect image or talk about your flaws? How open will you be? How will you react to criticism and opposing views? Ask yourself these questions and more.

Work to establish trust right from the onset. This means being true to your word. Don't promise things you can't deliver and don't endorse products that will harm your brand. Also, don't shy away from bad reviews or different viewpoints. You can learn a lot from people who criticize your business. Use the experience to create better products and offer better services.

Build your customer base

One way to ensure you have a steady flow of income is to have customers that will buy from you again and again. This is your customer base. These are the people you aim to serve even as you look for more customers. You'd want to listen to them, provide solutions to their problems and reward them for their loyalty. Moreover, remember that you don't need a huge customer base in order to be successful, you just need a very active one.

But how exactly can you get customers?

Step 4: Traffic Is The Key

Traffic is the key. Why? Because without traffic you'll have almost no sales. As I mentioned before, you need to create content. But without traffic, it's all useless. So now your goal is to get traffic to your blog/website. Getting buyers is not easy, you need to build a connection, a relationship with them.

The first way is Google. Google is a search engine, and people go to Google to get info. Google has a lot of traffic and Google loves content. Having high-quality content is a positive thing in the eyes of Google. Google can identify if your content is relevant to the keywords that people search for. But don't just write content for content sake. Instead, try to be helpful. Give your visitors reason to stick around and come back again.

The second is using YouTube. YouTube is also a search engine. You can give a deeper level of value with YouTube, so it is quality traffic. Being able to rank your videos is similar to using Google to rank your site. The most important thing is to optimize your title and use keywords. Make sure to use links in your description.

Social media (Facebook, Instagram, Twitter, Pinterest, Google+, etc.) is an incredible asset. Again, the key is to have high-quality content. Share as much as you can. You can share personal things too. Try to engage your visitors and share your content with their friends. Also, keep in mind that every post you share doesn't have to be a sales pitch. You can share useful information and links or articles about other blogs or products that would be of some value to your visitors.

Using podcasts is quite a new and powerful way because people can use a podcast while they're doing different things. A podcast is an audio file. It's not as competitive as the other options.

You can publish Kindle books on Amazon very inexpensively. You can put it up for $0.99 and you can get thousands of downloads. In your Kindle book, you can link to your website or product. The only way to communicate to your readers later is to funnel them to your website. Make sure to have high-quality content in your Kindle book and give value for your readers. Build a relationship with them and provide value.

Doing an interview with other people can also get traffic to you. A guest blog is also can help you, just post something relevant to the blog. These are just other bonus strategies.

If you already have visitors, you can communicate with them via email, and you can send them to your blog/website over and over again. Later on, I will explain in more detail how you can build an email list.

There are also paid traffic methods like Facebook ads. With Facebook, you can target. But I don't recommend this in the beginning. Try to keep your cost low in the beginning. Later if you have a lot of profit, you can spend on advertising, but until then, try to get free traffic.

These are the basic strategies, but you can learn more about getting traffic if you'd like. I advise following Digital Marketer. You can learn a lot from them about internet marketing. I just want to give you a big overview about this. In the next chapter, I will explain more advanced strategies.

To sum up, getting value isn't about selling, it's about adding value and helping people. Don't be afraid to give high-value stuff for free. It will return to you.

Step 5: How To Create An Online Business

In this chapter, you will read an incredible strategy, the core thing to create a successful and profitable online business. This strategy is known as sales funnel. Maybe you heard about it before. You can use this for any kind of business.

The first step is free stuff. Giveaway something for free. It can be a blog post, a YouTube video, a podcast. Most people like videos, it's a very powerful way to start. Give your visitor a step-by-step guide or some useful tips, advice. It must be high value as you want them to buy from you. If they get very high-quality content for free, they will buy your products because they will know that it will also be high quality, because they already trust you, like you, and connect with you. So get them on your email list with this free giveaway. You'll give this free stuff in exchange for their email address.

The next step is the front-end offer. After you get your visitor's email address, survey them. What would they like? What challenges do they have? They will tell you what they want, what their challenges are. So you will know what can be your front-end offer. Don't be afraid. People would rather buy a product than search for solutions for their problems for hours. I know that all information is available for free on the internet, but people don't want to spend so much time searching for this information. This front-end offer can be an ebook, a video course, etc. You don't have to give it away for free but try to keep the price low. You can create more front-end offers that funnel into your core offer, which is the next step.

After that, sell the core offer. This is something that's a more advanced training program. In your front-end offer you give some basic tips and information, but in your core offer, you have to give something of higher value—a step-by-step ultimate training program. The price of this can be higher because they trust you more after your front-end offer.

The next part is the up sell. This is more advanced training. This will help your customer take it to the next level. This is for people who want more from you. This is something which isn't covered in the more basic products. The up sell price is higher, but it depends on the market you're in. You can use a reoccurring fee on a monthly basis.

The next piece is cross promotion. This is for further serving your customers. Cross promotion is selling other products/services that can help them. This product/service can be your own product, but you can share other people's products as well. That is called affiliate marketing, but I will tell you more about it later.

The final piece is coaching and consulting. However, this is active income, not passive. So there will be a need for your coaching but don't offer this for everyone because your time is limited. You can charge a lot more per hour for it.

A sales funnel is also useful for getting traffic, because people will find your free offer.

It all starts with a free giveaway. This will cost you money and time, but you need to offer it for free or inexpensively. Why is it good for you? Because after that you're able to promote more things. So start with the front-end, but the money is in the backend. The majority of people don't buy, they just want free stuff. That's okay, but a lot of people want more. They will buy. They are very valuable. Your task is to find your niche's problem and provide a solution to them. If someone buys from you a high-value product/service, they'll want to buy more from you. They want more. So offer them more and help them achieve more. You need to work on creating more products. Create more solutions that can help your customer so that you can build a sales funnel, a backend.

Step 6: Adding Value

I know I talked a lot about adding value, but because this is the most important thing in a business, I want to talk about it even more.

Don't be afraid to put out content. Don't be a perfectionist. Even if your content isn't perfect, ask a question to yourself: is it adding value, can people benefit from it? If the answer is yes, then just put it out there, because it will help people. Make a difference and help people with your content to change their life.

Keep improving yourself to be able to add more and more value. Your goal is to have a lot of followers, to have followers who want to learn more from you. Trust me, they will come, they will find you.

Stop focusing on you, focus on other people. Don't focus on making money, focus on adding value first. If you start adding value, people will be grateful for that, and later they will give money for your courses/coaching.

I personally recommend making YouTube videos. At first, nobody will see them, but if you add value, more and more people will find you. After you have some subscribers, they will engage with you and your videos will rank better and better. So the key is to add value and create a lot of content. At the beginning try to record a video at least once a week. Don't let people forget about you.

Create a lot of videos around one keyword. Research as much as you can. Create "how to" videos for keywords that people are searching for. Optimize your content for that keyword. After a time, you don't have to use keywords when you have an audience. Make a list of your topic ideas and create as much content as you can. Remember, the more the better, and this will attract people to you. Try different things in the beginning. At the end of your videos, ask people to subscribe to your channel, or say "leave a comment below,"—this is a call to action. If they enjoyed your videos and benefited from them, they will follow you. Focus on serving, focus on creating high-quality content, so more and more people will watch your videos.

If you want to avoid failure, you need to constantly evolve, improve, and add value. So your goal is to add more value than anyone else. Don't be afraid, just be yourself. You will find people who are your customer for life because they will be so passionate about you and your brand. Your main goal is not to create customers, but fans, because this is more valuable. A one-time customer gives short-time success, but creating a fan is long-term. Think about Apple. Apple has fans. They are fans of the brand. They buy feelings, not products. That's why Apple has so many buyers who buy almost every year when Apple creates something brand new. Apple always adds value, always finds a way to achieve success, always finds a way to give incredible value.

Step 7: Marketing Tips

Marketing means many things. Maybe the best definition is to attract people to you. How can you use the internet to get more customers/clients?

First, you need a website with a call to action. Make sure that this website converts visitors into customers. Your only work will be to send traffic to this website. Remember, at the first moment you don't want to sell, you want to giveaway free stuff and collect their email addresses.

Facebook ads, Facebook PPC (paid per click advertising), Facebook fan page, Google Adwords (Google advertisement option), SEO (search engine optimization), YouTube, Twitter, Instagram, LinkedIn, and Pinterest can all help you to attract people to your website. You can search for blog posts related to your topic and simply leave a comment with a link to your site. This is a powerful strategy as you use someone else's traffic and lead them to your webpage. You can use a lot of different opportunities to send traffic to your website. My advice is to use one strategy first and once you have mastered it, select another one and so on. Use marketing to build your brand.

Okay, so how do you sell once you attract people to you? First of all, you need confidence that your product is quality and it will make money. People buy from people who they know, like, and trust. You need to work on getting to know the person and building a relationship with them. Identify what their problems are to be able to serve them. Survey them, ask them what their problems are. The relationship and trust are very powerful. You need to make sure that there is a need for your product.

People buy things from emotion. There are the two motivators: pain and pleasure. Offer something to avoid pain or to give pleasure. Of course, pain is a stronger motivator. Use some kind of call to action and use a good headline. Not everybody will say yes, but that's okay. Keep trying to sell people. Ask people about their excuse. Sell something you would buy too. Don't sell worthless stuff.

Let me give you some pricing strategy. Price depends on the value that you offer. Starting small is always a good idea. The more demand, the more money you can charge. If you start small, you make more people interested, so then you can sell your product at a higher price. However, every market is different. Look around and compare your price with your competitors' price. The simple answer is the more value you give, the more money you'll make.

Marketing is all about finding a way to get your products out there. You need to promote a lot, reach as many people as you can, sell them as much as you can and improve this process as much as you can. Always try new things. Don't use the same marketing strategies. You don't want to miss out. Learn the new trends and adapt them. If something doesn't work, find another way to sell.

Step 8: Examples Of Online Money Making Opportunities

Okay, now you know how to find your niche, how to build your brand, get traffic, do marketing and so on. This is the foundation. You can't make money without these things. But how can you make money after you do all this? What kind of opportunities exist? Let's take a look.

You can sell physical products through a lot of websites like Amazon or Ebay meaning you should have an inventory. This costs money, however, if you buy a large quantity, you can buy items cheaper.

Another opportunity is publishing ebooks, paperback books, and audio books. You can write your own book or hire someone to do it for you. You can hire freelancers or find a writing company to write you a book. Then just publish your book on any platform, like Amazon Kindle, and make money after every sale. You can even hire a graphics designer to do the cover for you too. If you'd like to publish your ebook on Amazon Kindle, you just need a KDP account which is free to use, and you will get a royalty (depending on the price of your book) after every sale you make.

The next option is advertisement. If you have a popular blog or YouTube channel, you can advertise something related to your niche for a high amount of money. You can find people who need a popular website to advertise his/her product, or you can use Google AdSense and make money from it.

Affiliate marketing is a good thing if you don't have your own product. Affiliate marketing means that you sell other people's products for a commission. Your task is to lead traffic to their sales page, and if a customer buys the product/service, you earn a commission from that. There are some amazing websites full of affiliate marketing opportunities, like Clickbank.

You can create information products and sell them as your own product. However, it requires a lot of time and effort, but the investment can be returned. If you know so much about a topic, you're free to do a digital product about it. However, you should learn a lot before doing this.

The next option is to make a software or mobile app. It can cost you a lot of money unless you're a software developer. You can put your mobile app on the Apple App Store and offer it for free or charge for every download. If you choose to give it away for free, you can make money while people use that app, for example, you can sell something inside the app.

We've already talked about it, but services can be another opportunity. For instance, you can offer coaching and consulting or be a freelancer. That's another option to make money online. If you're an expert in something and you have a lot of followers, there will be a need for your much deeper help. I would like to draw your attention, though, because these aren't passive income sources.

Except forservices, all of the above options are passive income sources. This means that you need to work hard and put your energy and money into it in thebeginning, but after that, you're able to automate it almost 100%. Coaching/consulting and freelancing require your time, so these are active income sources. However, you can work from anywhere, which means these provide a certain freedom too.

Step 9: How To Grow Your Online Business

Now I'll share with you a few tips which will allow you to grow your business. Of course, this isn't for beginners. These are more advanced tips. If you are just starting with your business, it isn't relevant to you. However, it can give you an idea of where you need to go. Remember, you need to work as hard as you can at the beginning, but later, you won't want to work your ass off any longer. You want to automate your business as much as possible. Okay, so I'll give the three most important things.

At the beginning, you have to do everything. At the beginning,you work in the business. That's okay because at first, you don't have the money to hire someone. However, you have to hire virtual assistants (VAs) later on. You'll need help. Hire people that are better than you. That's very important because later you need to work *on* your business, not *in* your business. Be a business owner, a manager, and have a team. This is the end goal. Don't waste your time on tasks that anybody else can do. Focus on tasks that you can't outsource, like creating content. At the beginning, you can hire freelancers or companies who have a team in place. You can find people on Upwork for constant tasks, or you can use Fiverr.com to outsource ad hoc tasks.

Having virtual assistants are good because you can easily train them to do things so you'll have more time. You can use that time to build more businesses. We talked about online moneymaking opportunities already—use your time and build multiple businesses. Try to automate as many things as possible. You can even use all the discussed options to make money online. Think big and diversify your income. That's the most secure way. Don't use only one opportunity. Don't put all your eggs in one basket. I recommend buildingas many online businesses as you can around your brand.

Cross promote your existing products. If you have a publishing business and a physical business too, that's great. Make a book on a certain topic and promote one of your physical products in it. You can promote your information product too in your book. Affiliate marketing is powerful. You're free to use it in every business. You can always offer other peoples' products if they are relevant to the topic and can give value to your customer. The goal is a win-win-win situation. Win for you, your customers, and the owner of the product. Be creative and use cross promotion to make more money.

Some More Useful Online Business Tips

Before we jump into these amazing advanced tips, let me thank you and congratulate you on reading the book all the way through. I really appreciate it. Let's take a look at some more advanced tips.

We talked a lot about giving value. This is the core thing. As an entrepreneur, your task is to serve people and give as much value as you can. So don't do the bare minimum. Always offer bonuses with your products/services. This will attract more people because they'll think that they'll get higher value for the same amount of money. It creates more sales.

A lot of people think they have plenty of time. That's why they always postpone a purchase. Avoid this. Having a time limit pressures people to buy—that's exactly what you need. Use a counter on your sales page. You can say that your product won't be available after the time expires or it will be available at a higher price. Trust me, people most likely will buy if they know that your offer is a limited time offer and won't be available anymore at the same price. They think they're saving money, so they will buy before the time expires.

Be unique. Don't sell one single product/service. Make a whole package with a lot of offers in it so that it can't be compared with your competition's products.

The next tip is to narrow down your niche. If you choose a subniche, people will more likely feel that your product is exactly for them. I've already explained what subniches are, but think about a product called "sales training" and think about one called "sales training for online entrepreneurs". Which one would you choose? See? It has amazing power. Choose a narrow niche in your product names.

Another great strategy is the money back guarantee. There will be a lot of people who'll have doubts about your product. If you want to turn those visitors into customers, you'll need to offer a money back guarantee. Trust me, very few people will redeem the guarantee, but it will get a lot more buyers, so it's totally worth it. Again, be unique. If your competitor provides a 100% 30-day money back guarantee, you should offer more. Maybe you should provide a 110% money back guarantee. This will help you to get more customers. Remember, if you make high-quality content, very few people will redeem the guarantee.

Writing a sales letter requires a lot of expertise. However, there are a few basic tips you can apply. First of all, use testimonials. This will help to dispel doubts. Try to handle fears and write down how your product can help them. Ask customers what they need and provide it to them. They need to feel that your product is created exactly for them. Use text and a video format too as there will be people who want to watch the video and there will be people who just want to read through your page.

Conclusion

Thank you again for buying this book!

I hope this book was able to help give you a big overview of how can you build a successful and sustainable online business that can create financial freedom. But please remember that passive income doesn't come by itself. You need to be patient and work hard. As long as you have the desire, the motivation, you can achieve whatever you want. It doesn't matter what circumstances you're in. Don't let anything stop you. If there is somebody who can make it, you can make it too. Find a way to make passive income and use this amazing opportunity called the internet.

The next step is to take action. One little final tip I'll give you is that the best time to take action or apply things is right after you learn something. If you leave it until later, if you think "Okay, I'll apply these things, but first I'll do this, this and this" then you know what happens? Yes, you're never going to get it done. So please schedule time right now. Trust me, if you apply what you learn right now, that's what is going to get you the result, because your motivation is the highest at this moment.

You remember everything now, so you can make a lot of progress. You can take massive action right now. So start working on your online business.

If you need more motivation, just remember your goal. As long as you take consistent action, you will be making more money, and you will have a better life and more freedom because of it. I want to encourage you to take massive action, apply the things you've just learned, commit yourself and set goals now. Hopefully, you were taking notes. Review them and just set up some action steps that you can take moving forward.

Did you learn something new? I hope so. Then let's apply that and take action with that. That's really my hope for you—not to read passively, but actually apply what I shared with you because as long as you do, you'll make money and you'll become successful, and that's really what I want for you.

Are you still reading this book? Okay, now you can stop reading and start taking massive action. That's the most important thing. Really think about how you can take action based on this and work your ass off because that's the only way that you are going to get to where you want to go. It's not easy, but with hard work and commitment, which I know you have, you will get there. I'm confident that you will.

If I have to give you a final tip then I would say just take consistent action, always be learning and improving yourself. Sometimes, you're going to have to make sacrifices. It is going to be hard and challenging but as long as you have that mentality of finding a way and committing yourself to it, then you will be successful, and you will get to where you want to go.

I really want to just push you a little bit further than what you thought you could do before and just keep going down this path because it can be a very fulfilling path. The internet can provide so much opportunity, and there are so many ways to make money from it. I can promise you'll be better tomorrow than where you are today, as long as you keep taking action and you keep making progress. It's just an incredible gift that we've been given with the internet and what it can provide for us.

If you apply the things you have learned, the sky is the limit. Anything is possible with this. It's just about applying yourself. Take action with it, scale it up, and keep doing it. As long as you do that, I have no doubt that you will be extremely successful with this. I want to really encourage you to keep going. Reward yourself for the progress. Make sure you reward yourself and celebrate that because it's going to allow you to do more. It's going to motivate you to want to do more of that. It's going to pull you.

I Need Your Help...

Finally, if you enjoyed this book, then I'd like to ask you for a favor, would you be kind enough to leave a review for this book on Amazon? It'd be greatly appreciated!

I want to reach as many people as I can with this book, and more reviews will help me accomplish that!

www.ingramcontent.com/pod-product-compliance
Lightning Source LLC
Chambersburg PA
CBHW071153220526
45468CB00003B/1037